I Care About
MY FAMILY

Liz Lennon

![CRABTREE logo]

CRABTREE
PUBLISHING COMPANY
WWW.CRABTREEBOOKS.COM

CRABTREE
PUBLISHING COMPANY
WWW.CRABTREEBOOKS.COM

Published in Canada
Crabtree Publishing
616 Welland Avenue
St. Catharines, ON
L2M 5V6

Published in the United States
Crabtree Publishing
347 Fifth Ave,
Suite 1402-145
New York, NY 10016

Published by Crabtree Publishing Company in 2021

Printed in the U.S.A./122020/CG20201014

Author: Liz Lennon

Editorial director: Kathy Middleton

Editors: Sarah Peutrill, Janine Deschenes

Design: Collaborate

Illustrator: Michael Buxton

Proofreader: Melissa Boyce

Production coordinator
& Prepress technician: Samara Parent

Print coordinator: Katherine Berti

Library and Archives Canada Cataloguing in Publication

Title: I care about my family / Liz Lennan.
Other titles: My family
Names: Lennon, Liz (Children's non-fiction writer), author. | Buxton, Michael (Artist), illustrator.
Description: Illustrated by Michael Buxton. |
  Previously published: London: Franklin Watts, 2020. | Includes index.
Identifiers: Canadiana (print) 20200357204 | Canadiana (ebook) 20200357271 |
  ISBN 9781427128911 (hardcover) |
  ISBN 9781427128973 (softcover) |
  ISBN 9781427129031 (HTML)
Subjects: LCSH: Families—Juvenile literature.
Classification: LCC HQ744 .L46 2021 | DDC j306.85—dc23

Library of Congress Cataloging-in-Publication Data

Names: Lennon, Liz (Children's non-fiction writer), author. |
  Buxton, Michael (Artist), illustrator.
Title: I care about my family / Liz Lennon ; illustrated by Michael Buxton.
Other titles: My family
Description: New York, NY : Crabtree Publishing Company, 2021. |
  Series: I care about | First published in Great Britain in 2020 by the Watts Publishing Group.
Identifiers: LCCN 2020045683 (print) | LCCN 2020045684 (ebook) |
  ISBN 9781427128911 (hardcover) |
  ISBN 9781427128973 (paperback) |
  ISBN 9781427129031 (ebook)
Subjects: LCSH: Families--Juvenile literature.
Classification: LCC HQ744 .L46 2021 (print) | LCC HQ744 (ebook) |
  DDC 306.85--dc23
LC record available at https://lccn.loc.gov/2020045683
LC ebook record available at https://lccn.loc.gov/2020045684

Contents

What is a family?

A family is a group of people who love, trust, and care about each other. They usually live in a home together. Sometimes a family is made up of children living with their two parents. Other families are made up of children with one parent, grandparents, and other caregivers. Some families have many children, while others have none. Families can be big or small.

Who is in your family?

This is Lola's family tree. A family tree shows all of the members in a family. Lines show how the members are related. Lola has two parents, a brother, and a sister. They all live in a house together. Lola also has grandparents, aunts, an uncle, and a cousin. They don't live with Lola.

Your family tree

What does your family tree look like?

You could make a family tree by drawing pictures of your family or using photos.

Start with your grandparents, then your parents and their siblings. Finally, add yourself, your siblings, and your cousins. Everyone's family tree is different.

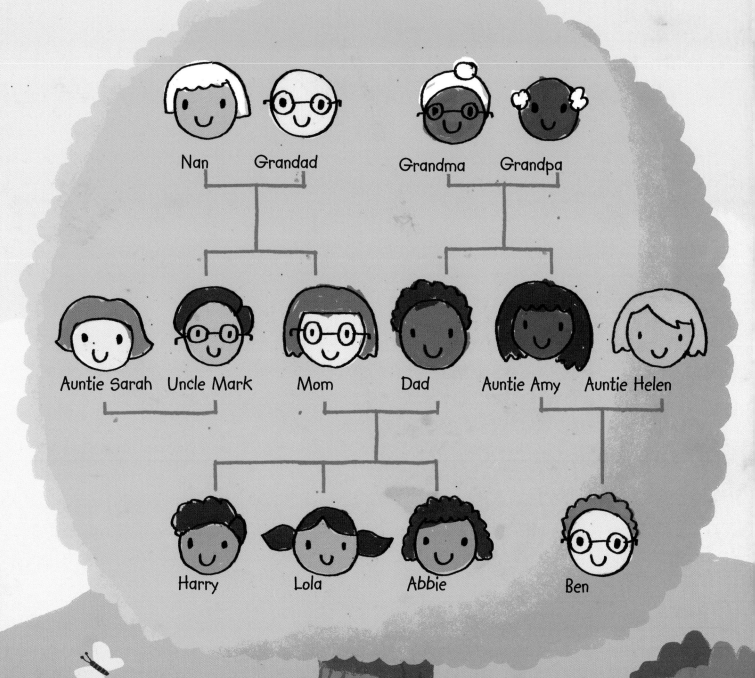

Caring families

The most important job family members do is care for each other. Parents give their children food, shelter, and clothing. They show their children love and help them grow up to be happy and **confident**. This is an important job, but it's not an easy one. It's a little like looking after a vegetable garden. It takes a lot of time and care. Slowly, the vegetables grow healthy and strong.

Healthy and happy

Parents and caregivers set rules with their children. They need to make sure their children brush their teeth, eat their vegetables, and get enough sleep—even when they do not want to. Parents do these things to help their children be healthy and happy.

Can you think of rules made by your parents and caregivers to help you stay healthy and happy?

Happy times

Families often enjoy spending time together.

Some families like going to the park or taking a walk.

Other families play games, create art, and cook.

On special days and holidays, many families do fun things together. They may have parties and make certain foods.

Many enjoy special family **traditions**.

Think about it

How does your family have fun together?

How does your family celebrate holidays?

Everyday life

Families also do everyday **chores** that might not be as much fun. These tasks might include going to work and school, going grocery shopping, and doing household chores such as cooking meals and cleaning. When family members work together, chores can be easier—and might be a little more fun!

Think about it

How can you be helpful when your parents or caregivers have chores to do?

Can you think of a way to make an everyday chore more fun?

13

Love and Kindness

Every day we should show love
and Kindness to our families.
Here are some ways family
members show these things.

Making
meals

Giving hugs

Reading
together

14

Teaching new skills

Playing games

Think about it

How do your family members show you love and kindness?

How do you show you care for your family?

15

Your caregivers

People who care for children have many tasks to do! They need to take care of children by providing food, shelter, and love. They also have to look after themselves and, sometimes, other family members.

They must be like superheroes!

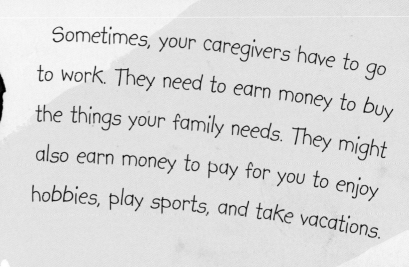

Sometimes, your caregivers have to go to work. They need to earn money to buy the things your family needs. They might also earn money to pay for you to enjoy hobbies, play sports, and take vacations.

Think about it

Do your parents or caregivers go to work?

How can you show your parents or caregivers that you are thankful for the things they buy for you?

17

Brothers and sisters

Some children have brothers or sisters. Your siblings can be wonderful friends who support you and share interests with you. Siblings often have to share toys, books, and even bedrooms. Sharing isn't always easy! Sometimes, we just want all of the pizza for ourselves! Many children do not have siblings. They learn to share with friends and other family members.

Think about it

What do you have in common with your siblings? If you don't have siblings, think about friends or other family members. What differences do you have with your siblings?

What ways can you share and get along with your siblings more easily?

19

Family arguments

Everyone feels angry with their family members sometimes. Parents may feel frustrated when they are in a hurry and trying to get to work. Children may feel upset when a sibling borrows a toy or a parent insists they follow a rule. Being angry or frustrated can feel like you have a grumpy monster inside.

Try this

Next time a family member seems angry or frustrated, try to think about what they are feeling and why. How could you help them feel better?

Making up

When we argue with our family, the best way
to show we care is to apologize. It's not always easy to
apologize when we feel angry. To calm down, try taking
deep breaths. Count slowly to 10.

There are different ways to apologize. You can show you
are sorry by doing a kind act for a family member. You can
give a hug or write a note. You can tell your family member
that you are sorry. Apologizing also means that you will try
not to do the same thing again.

Family near and far

We see the family members we live with every day. But sometimes we have family we don't live with. They may live far away and we may not see them often. You can show you care about family members far away too. You can talk on the phone or video chat. You can make a card to send by mail. These actions show others that we are thinking about them.

Changing families

Families are always changing. Children grow up and learn to do new things. New brothers and sisters are born. Families might move to new houses, cities, or even countries! Sometimes, there are difficult and sad changes such as parents splitting up or the death of a grandparent.

If you are upset or worried about a change in your family, talk to a trusted adult about how you feel. Telling people how you feel allows them to help you feel better. Remember that changes such as parents splitting up are never your fault.

27

All kinds of families

Every family is different. They each have different rules, traditions, and ways of doing things. Some families **value** their religion or faith. Many make their **culture** a big part of everyday life, from food to clothing and holidays. Other families don't follow a religion, but have beliefs and traditions they value.

18

13

10

8

7

Think about it

Wouldn't the world be boring if everyone was the same? Try to learn about the things other families do together. Remember to always treat other people with respect. It is normal for other families to do things differently than your family.

Remember...

There are all kinds of families. Some people have siblings and some don't. Some people have one parent and others have two.

Families have fun together, but sometimes there are also chores and important things to do.

Being in a family means sharing things.

All families have different rules and traditions.

There are many ways to show our family members that we care.

Sometimes, family members argue with each other. Apologizing is a good way to make up.

Words to Know

chores Small jobs that people do on a regular basis, such as washing clothes and dishes

confident Feeling happy in yourself and open to trying new things

culture The customs, traditions, and arts of a group of people

tradition Practices and beliefs that are passed down from generation to generation

value To believe that something is important and morally right

Index